At The *Eleventh* Hour

COPYRIGHT INFORMATION

AT THE ELEVENTH HOUR

Copyright © 2024 by O'Shea" D. Myles

Published 2024 by Eagle Peak Entertainment, LLC

Cover design: Eagle Peak Entertainment, LLC
Cover art copyright © Marco Lim Canillas

At The Eleventh Hour is a book of poetry and a work of fiction. Any resemblance to actual events, places, incidents, or persons, living or dead, is entirely coincidental.

All rights reserved.

No part of this book may be used or reproduced in any manner whatsoever without the express written permission of the publisher, except for the use of brief quotations in a book review.

ISBN: 979-8-9921646-0-2

DEDICATION

This book is dedicated to my wife Eko Canillas-Myles who never gave up on me and inspired the love that created the remembering poems. To my family whose strong foundation allowed me to find my voice. To my son whose questioning nature and adventurous spirit always pushed me to go deeper. To my father who said if you want to be a writer then you must write every day. To my mother Jackie who asked me to write her a poem every birthday. To my mother Karon who made sure I passed my English class so that I could write. To my high school English teacher who told me to write what I know. Especially to my grandmother Muffin, the first writer I ever knew, my inspiration and my north star, who has always been and will always be my champion.

ACKNOWLEDGEMENT

To my editor Desa Philadelphia for her expertise, support, belief, and encouragement, for without her this book would have never made it off my shelf. Her insightful feedback and dedication served to shape and nurture this collection.

CONTENTS

Emerging…
Not all who wander roam
Childhood
Slow Clap
Seasons
Intravenous
Out of Sight
Too Much
Mad Mad World
One Breath
The Best
Wag The Dog
Trick
Hiding
All or Nothing
Encouragement
Unbinds
Ending Soul
Another Life
Between Us
Awake
Timing
Freedom
Lessons

Remembering Love…
L.O.V.E
Beautiful Thoughts
A Womyn
Chocolate
Ecstasy
Glazed
Toast
Purpose
Meet Cute
Whispers
Again
View from the Balcony
Brought to Life
The Whole World
One
Uninventable Beauty
Heart and Soul
Excuses
Anyone Else
Broken
Losing Her
Dreamland
Mistake
Be Myself
That's it, That's all

Laid Bare…
Been There
Perceptive
C R A C K S
Waiting for the Unknown
Idolatry as Fame
The National Nation
Excuse me
This Time
Because We Are One
Heavy
Living On
Believe In Me
Cycle
As Me
Time
NO
What Then
Picture This
Champion
Unnecessary
The Gift
The Eleventh Hour
Emerging

INTRODUCTION

The Eleventh Hour is a reflection of the past, a commentary on the present and a hope for the future. Each section representing before the pandemic, during the pandemic and the aftereffects of the pandemic. The book in its entirety is a life laid bare and a reflection on the times we are in and a history that cannot seem to help but repeat itself. Although set during a specific place in time; the words, stories, and scenarios -- speak to a pattern of the human condition, need for connection, need for validation and screaming into a void forever wishing to be heard.

Intense with biting criticism of itself and the world it was born into; this collection speaks to the anger, frustration, love, and realization of the hope humanity strives to be. Ideas that fight to become more of themselves and open up conversation about what was, what is, and what can or should be. The note under the note and the truth between the lines. This book opens up a meta space in the universe in order to look upon itself and question its own reality.

This book is for those who wonder why, if, and how. Those who question the question to the answer they thought they found. Who wonder how and where they fit, those who lost hope and still wonder why they haven't left yet. For those whose voice has not found it's place. For those who have lost all sense of time and space, where anger and despair have all but replaced. For those who are looking for an honest reflection of our time and most of all a hopeful take.

Before I knew it my life had changed, living in isolation, and fearing death at every phase. I tried remembering love since fear, greed, anger, and foolishness worked so hard to take that away. Then exhausted, frustrated, and seemingly defeated I laid bare all that I had been afraid to say. Naked and unashamed, at the eleventh hour I made my peace.

This book is a letting go, this book is keeping track, this book is remembering what we had, what we lost, what we've gained and what we still lack. This book is an honesty about our systems that are cracked and our slow and painful journey to finding our way back.

At The *Eleventh* Hour

O'Shea" Myles

A BOOK OF POETRY

At The Eleventh Hour…

Emerging

Not all who wander roam

Sadness leads to overwhelm
death rings its forever bell

Shall I answer
I know not

The bells ring
lately, quite a lot

Compassion took a trip
to a place long forgot

Where free souls roam, nature's grown
Fear regrets and peace is home

Courage got off the train
before the spot

I didn't even notice
until the last stop

Location nowhere
destination home
ticket to a better place

Not all who wander roam

Childhood

A sad face
a tear

One second
one year

One shoe hanging from a line

A handprint in cement
not so hard to find

The smell of grass
the taste of dew

A mattress in an alley
a fence between me and you

A broken-down roof
a makeshift pigeon coop

Fresh greens in the garden
cumquats on the tree

Memories grow weary
of what use to be

Slow Clap

I am not to blame for the darkness of others
yet I am the canvas they choose to paint
their bloody masterpiece upon

I hang myself atop a wall for all to see
they continually walk by, blind, at ease
I alone stand, the audience is me

A slow clap for the bloody masterpiece

Seasons

Rolling green hills
sparkling blue water
swings that reach the sky

Sand gets in your eye
shade falls from trees

Dancing in fallen leaves

Hide and go seek
versus
Hide and go get it

Fun and games until you have to kiss it

Chili cheese Fritos
don't be late or you'll miss it

Friends and neighbors
owed things and favors

The longest nights
The hottest days

Growing up faster
than time has paid

Intravenous

The lies I've told myself
Are more truth than fiction
Feed to me intravenously
To the point of being sickening

For what I could not do for myself
They graciously offered to do for me
Not the lead I got to play
But a side note in my own story

The greatest dream I could have been
For those who came before me
Systems, doors, and painted whores
barriers as distraction laid bare

Inequity as ecstasy, so little do I care
Disappearing history, future as a mystery
Unsolved in a lonely, blank, stare

What lives really matter?

Out of sight

Every time I close my eyes
I wish I could see more

For time, like shadows wait for me
Through life's revolving doors

In and out, around and through
Absent ceilings, missing floors

The key to free each waking dream
Lies in the one before

Too Much

So much to say
So little time
So much to do
So little mine
So much to think
So vast my mind
So bored in this world
So much to find
So much need
So little to be kind
So much beauty
So wasted on pride
So much love
So many denied
So much happiness
So hard to find
So much everything
So never enough
So much waste
So many lies
So much sadness
      So much misaligned
So many missed the boat
So many, too tired to try
So much isolation
So much on my mind
So much frustration
So much on the line
So much to lose
So, a little here and there seems fine…

Mad Mad World

There is a madness afoot
that burns off my lashes
and hurts my eyes

There is a madness afoot
that torches my soul
and is full of lies

There is a madness afoot
that binds my soul
and makes me cry

There is a madness afoot
that brings about the end of days
and makes the streets run blood red with wine

There is a madness afoot
that makes sense of this loss of time
and pretends that everything is fine

There is a madness afoot
that I forgot her place or mine
and was it a dream, a zoom, or a lie

There is a madness afoot
that I constantly question the validity of my mind
and questioning reality, is the new reality, of our time

There is a madness afoot
that the loss of all sense seems fine
and sense making is a pastime of a long past time

There is a madness afoot
that isolation is the friend I beg to be kind
and seeking so much outside myself… is death the only friend I find

There is a madness afoot
that true madness makes a fool of mine
and in a mad, mad, world madness is the only calm I find…

One Breath

The Sun
The Moon
The Ocean
The Stars
The Dirt
The Mud
The Rocks
The Yard
The House
The Laundry
The Trash
The Cars
The Driveway
The Porch
The Street
The Bar
The Store
The Bedroom
The Bath
The Bus
The School
The Class
The Room
The Lunch
The Sandbox
The Cemetery
The Casket
The Church
The Cave
The Earth
The Basinet
And the Birth

From the cradle
To the grave
Some life
Still left to

Unearth…

The Best

Patience is a thing
I can hardly wait for

Gate keepers
Closed doors
I do not need permission

Patience for myself?

A weight is lifted
Knowing I'm, only waiting
For my best

Wag The Dog

Helicopters circle like
Cockroaches around shit

Searching lights move like
Rats through alleys
Scouring for scraps

Crazy Karen's cause malfeasance
Destroying any sense of
Serve and Protect

Army trucks roll down streets
Calming inequities created by police
Violence and fear their bullet proof vest

If the tail always wags the dog
Then what's next?

Trick

Solo in my old age
Still young enough
To voice my rage

Peaceful
Mind full of mess
Trying and failing
To do my best

Always a test
That I gave myself
Grade myself
My voice grating
In my ear

Full of wax
Can barely hear
Screaming voices
Try to get out
Too much energy here

Fear I mastered,
Tried to master me
A fight to the death
Unequal test

If I was to lose
Then sleep no more
Til death

What test
Past, fast, alas
I am what is left

Choosing not
To be defeated
My greatest trick yet

Hiding

Freedom tried to find me
But for years I ran away

It chased me through alleys
Backyards, houses, and hideaways

It found me in school
Then got buried under lies

It found me in love
Then went to sleep and closed it eyes

It found me in solace
Then destruction came

It found me in the bedroom
Then I forgot its name

It found me in the written word
Then I lost the page

It found me in the quiet moments
Until it met my rage

It found me in compassion
Until the day I was betrayed

It found me in my joy
Until sadness took its place

It found me through my voice
Then fear took that away

It found me through my art

It finally stopped looking

…That part!

All or Nothing

All I know is that I know nothing
And if that is anything
Then that is something

Encouragement Unbinds

Walked, I did, the mountain of discontent
And still, I am not discouraged

Raise my hand and was named Maleficent
And still, I am not discouraged

Hands locked in chains, a gang, made from many a barbed wire fence
And still, I am not discouraged

Blood of my ancestors… ancient, black, thick and still,
Still freshly dripping from their whips
And still, I am not discouraged

Devilish functions run free and unchecked
And still, I am not discouraged

Wounds never heal, freshly reopened with each new reveal
And still, I am not discouraged

For every ladder climbed another takes its place
And still, I am not discouraged

Slow death takes friends of mine
And still, I am not discouraged

Youth slips away like sand through hands
And still, I am not discouraged

Peace alludes society like rape meets piety
And still, I am not discouraged

Dissolution fuels violence and confusion
And still, I am not discouraged

Adult screams silence children to death
And still, I am not discouraged

The church of murder is called to order, we are all attending mass
And still, I am not discouraged

Masks breed false courage to do dastardly things
And still, I am not discouraged

Humanity lessens by the second, all we refuse to see
And still, I am not discouraged

The broken record of violence to establish peace
And still, I am not discouraged

The strong abuse the meek, lessons in domination ending in defeat
And still, I am not discouraged

Fear masked as arrogance, around every turn,
Never aware, their building burns
And still, I am not discouraged

Not an origin story, just one of many,
Our story, allow this story,
Labeled, defiled, burned alive and buried,
Remembered only as a foul story
And still, I am not discouraged

So let this end here, a true story
And still…

Ending Soul

Darkness sets like night on light
Energy of the body
Fight or flight

Can no longer see what's right
In front of me

Blind to what can be

Thought this was normal

Another Life

Lost inside someone else's life
Forgot who I was
Been like this all my life

My favorite color
My favorite food
My left and my right

Easy for devils to take advantage
Of an unused life

Waking up to thoughts not my own
So agreeable
I look to others to find my way home
Forever lost

Yet still I roam

Between Us

All that it means

We are all connected

Things are not

Always as they seem

The differences

That we focus on

Make it easier

Between us

The meaning

Awake

Ever lasting
Ever green
Awakening
Moments
Never seen

Dreaming many
A splendored thing
Away goes my head
Miracles float on beams

So high, look blindly
Believe what is not seen
No one and nothing is there
Truth lies in meaning

Teaming with tenacity
Fearing nothing
The ground drops
Beneath me

Do not believe
Everything
They tell you

You see…

Timing

One can waste so much
More than one is given
What seems endless
Only to vanish in an instant

Taken for granted
Abused, manipulated
Hidden in the recesses
Of things unforgiven

Missing, in motion, mistaken
Misread, misplaced, misspoken
Misinterpreted, mislead

A mister or a mistress
Of an empty, cold, bed
Leading or following
Alive or dead

The hourglass reflected
In your eyes
The sand draining
From your head

Arms click
Around and above
Sleep steady
In your stead

Fast calls the morning ahead

Freedom

What is freedom
But that moment
When responsibility is
Taken from without
And held within

What is freedom
But a fleeting moment
When we realize
Everything we want
To purchase
We already own, and then…

What is freedom
But a release
From all of our fears

What is freedom
But the sound
Of our own good advice
Grating on our ears

What is freedom
But facing the lack
Of courage
That has held us back
For years

What is freedom
But divine intervention
Knowing the truth
And changing the gears

What is freedom
But confidence
In knowing

Why we are still here

Lessons

Lesson learned through punishment taught
Wisdom gained for fearful thoughts

Blessings earned to miracles lost
Freedoms exercised during wars fought

Death experienced and lives bought
Dreams realized being imaginations fault

Beauty recognized so ugliness wrought
Strength manifested for weakness sought

History repeats so not all is lost

Remembering Love

L. O. V. E.

Letting go of

    Our expectations

Very aware of our own limitations

    Everyday understanding

We are but characters

    In LOVE'S imagination

Beautiful Thoughts

She, as beautiful as God's thoughts could ever be

She was
She is
The most
Beautiful thing
since then

There has never been a time
When she was not within my mind
The other day I saw her dance
I could feel it as she took my hand

Along the ocean floor we walked
Sand between our toes and wind on our faces
Never closer could we two be
As we dwell in each other's spaces

Contouring the lines of each other's faces
In our thoughts
Speaking without talking
Moving without walking

Breathing without wanting
Living without needing
Just Being
My other half and me

Love in my eyes has never been so sweet

She, as beautiful as God's thoughts could ever be

A Womyn

Womyn come walk with me
Womyn come talk with me
Womyn make me feel
Womyn are unreal

Steel drums beat like my heart when I see a Womyn
Wolves cry out in the dark like my fear of Womyn
The moon shines bright with no shame like when I'm with a
Womyn
Like salt water I run down cheeks as I become one of their tears
sharing the pain of
Womyn

If love was a game, then chess would be its name
I'm just a pawn in it, trying not to win it
Womyn play me like a bass guitar
With deep pulsating sounds
That swim in my head as I go around

I'm in love with a Womyn!

Chocolate Ecstasy

Brown bodies intertwined
Twisting and turning like a wall full of vines

Black berry juice nectar as sweet as wine

How fine, how fine is the time
When we close our eyes
And open up our minds

Breathing in your essence
Melting in your presence

Legs like the most delicate limbs of a tree
All natural in sandals

Walking with a confidence
That would bring Jehovah himself
To bow down at your knees

Oh Please! Oh Please!

Drowning in the deepness of your eyes
Looks like two stars shining
In the blackest of skies

Skin as soft as silk from Milan
Girl, you know you got it going on

Dancing in your rhythm
Feeling your jism

Don't know if I'm gonna make it
Can't shake it
Can't fake it

You shine so bright the sun itself stands in your shadow

Wake me please, cause I know I'm dreaming

Bodies on fire awake with desire
Steam coming from places we never knew existed

Twisted in the thought of your body can talk
Breathing you in to make me whole
One look at you and I'm 20 years old

Chew me up and spit me out
Girl that's what I'm talkin' bout

Touch me if you will
Feel me if you must
Though one kiss from you
And I feel I may bust

Ashes to Ashes and Dust to Dust

Glazed

Sitting in a room full of people
Yet my eyes only concentrate on you

Pushed and bumped by hundreds of people
But I am truly only touched by you

What is this madness
My mind in a daze

My sight forever lost
Inside your gaze

Toast

I want you like my morning drag
Deep inside me like a fag

When we are silent and loud at the same time
Like a jazz horn manipulating sound

Like sex sweat creating levels
Before we enter underground

Like sweet and savory smells from our kitchen
While we dance naked doing dishes

As if the moment even had a name
And I've never played my bongos the same

Red juices spread over the edge of that damn pot
Our special sauce for the spaghetti

Even as chaos surrounds us there is still, life

Toast, two glasses of red wine…

Purpose

Dull knife
Purposely sharpened teeth
Slices a heart
Leaves it in pieces

Sweet left-over peaches
The last dessert together
Sitting to Rotting
Day becomes Night

Arms of the clock
Watch
They tick
Talk

Only mistake

Spoke too late…

Meet Cute

You came into my life at the exact moment I needed you there
At our first conversation outside the club
You questioned the necessity of your jacket
I answered, the jacket adds style and is made to look good
Because you are in it

Innocent flirting began our friendship
Intellectually stimulated by you was I
Intoxicated and illuminated
By your very presence

Sitting across from you at the bar, the club, the café
Everyone thinking we were a couple
Me, never wanting to correct their mistake

In you I could only see Beauty
I knew I was falling in love

Even more when I got to know you

You, clever with your words, words
That spoken with such confidence
Left me salivating and hungry for more

More of your thoughts, Ideas, nonsense, passion, pleasure
Pleasure, even if not immediately satisfying
At least it was something new

New, like a new car, new money, new house
To me you were the new womyn in my life

Whispers

I love it when Womyn talk to me

Touch me
Feel me
Love me

Talk to me Womyn

I sit outside your protective space
Biding my time
And holding my place

I fantasize about bringing your soul
To a boiling point that your body cannot contain

Hands tremble with anticipation
Breath quickens while body is waiting

Tears well up to release emotion
Legs cross to hold back the motion

Can I talk to you?

Again

Blindsided was I by
Your beauty
Your voice
Your smile

Towards me you sent a kind eye
At first, I only recognized you
As a ghost from my past

The friendship I thought we had
Was nothing compared to what I see now

I see you as what you are
Sensual, Sexual, Beautiful, Brilliant, Alive
And you've seen me all along

You touch me in a way
That my heart loses its pace

And I have been left wanting

View From the Balcony

Outside a window
Underneath a balcony
A silhouette emerges
Caressed by a soft moonlight

Full is the heart of the one who sings
Though feelings are unrequited
There is still a feeling of need

Inspection comes at a later date
When feelings are questioned
And honesty arrives too late

One intellectualizes
While the other fantasizes

She looks deep inside her soul
And tries to fill what she sees as a hole

One feels, forever and ongoing passion
Immediately overflowing

The one, dances to loves rhythm and beat
The other, to her past pain, a reason to retreat

The one feeling defeat
Though freed, feeling emotional relief

Both experience a type of grief…

Brought To Life

Sweet lady, you are to me
A dream brought to life
A wish come true

Your sweetness reminds me
Of a love long forgotten

You have the ability
To make me smile
As well as cry

What I thought to be dead in me
Has now, at this moment
Come to life

At times we keep ourselves
Locked in memories of our past

Misery loves company
Is a play too often cast

But in your eyes
I see myself
As I truly am

The Whole World

The way dreams come to life
I wished for her to come to me

I thought her before I saw her
Manifested her in every way, shape, and form
But I was not ready

I needed time to be strong for her
At times I feel like I waited too long for her

In my heart she was always there
I wrote poems and songs for her
To hear through the air

Every path I took
Every choice I made
All made sense
When I met her that way

Every moment until that moment
Every day until that day
All just preparation for
How I met her that way

A puzzle incomplete
A poem unfinished
A film missing a frame
A song without a hook

All I had to do was see her
And when she spoke
My breath she took

I wished for
a funny girl, a witty girl
a loving girl, a sexy girl

a beautiful girl, a brilliant girl

And what I got was a womyn
What I got was the whole world!

One

When she lays her head
Between my chin and my shoulder

Her breath quietly on my breast
The smell of her hair
Attacking every sense of myself

We are one

Uninventable Beauty

What could not be created even in eternal life's imagination
Or manifest itself in the wildest of dreams

What an artists could only capture in a single suspended moment
Or the intensity behind what a single word could mean

All of nature's wonder captured in one tiny blade of grass
The laughter of a baby, the tear of a Womyn
The beating of a human heart

The simultaneity of cause and effect, seeing things in the world
As they build up and fall apart

Uninventable beauty – as a form, as an art

To dance, to sing, perchance to dream
To be a part of this thing we call – In Love

Heart and Soul

To judge beauty is to never truly know it

What makes her pretty, is it because she's thin?

Is it her eyes, her lips, her breasts, her skin
Or is it the way she carries herself
For true beauty comes from within

See, when I look at a womyn I fall in love with her smile
She fills my head and makes me think funny things

I fall in love with her thoughts, her imagination, she
So beautiful when she dreams

Underneath the covers when her feet rub my feet
As I wrap my body around hers
Our spirits are connected and
My soul feels complete

Let me see you in your sweats
Relaxing on the couch
Your hair all messed

You as you work to make your house
Match the way you feel inside

Close your eyes, take your hand, and put it upon my chest
You feel that – My heart beats to your soul's rhythm

This is Love

Love is the dream Beauty wants to become

Excuses

When I look at you with loving eyes
When I allow myself to feel
The feeling never subsides

I love you most when I love myself
I see your greatness shine
When thoughts of myself
Do not constantly cloud my mind

A work in progress love is
And we make progress everyday

I'm not so critical of you when I'm taking care of me
I am not so controlling when I accept the things I cannot change = YOU
And have the courage to change the things I can = ME
And the desire and wisdom to know the difference is PEACE

I listen to you more when I realize I don't always have to be heard
Word -- for -- word -- for -- word -- for – word

It is easier to forgive you once I've forgiven myself
I finally can feel you because I have opened up to self

I finally trust you because my own insecurity has left
I know I love you – for I have no excuses left

Anyone Else

Anyone else in the world but you
I could have had
Should have had
Would have had but for you

What for you
Lost myself
Exhaust myself
Why didn't I do better than you

Settled myself
Embedded myself
Entrenched and solidified myself
More of myself with you

Broken

Never would I ever believe that who I worked so hard to become would get so broken and lost

Never thought I would ever question my feelings like they were something that I bought

Never thought the feelings I had would become a passing memory, like loss

Never thought wanting to be and make you happy would come at such a cost

Never thought I wouldn't want to have you in my every moments thought

Never thought my connection to you could be lost

First love, first moment, first handhold, first kiss, first date, first argument, first time we missed each other like this

First cry, first laugh, first dinner, first date, first time we trusted, first night as a mate

For all those firsts, never thought it would end up this way

Losing Her

Now what to do?
Empty house, half shaped bed
What to do when memories of her won't leave my head?
So, I get up and fix the sink
Like I was always supposed to do
I water the grass every section, ten minutes each, even after the morning dew
I cook meals one day at a time and one step closer to you
I touch the doorknob that was always loose
Remembering that time you were locked in the bathroom
I get my toolbox out to fix it sitting right next to you

Each day a new day
And yet and still I get up
Knowing how much I will always miss you

Dreamland

She is to me like the support the sea
She catches all my falls
She is what I float upon
She is the wind beneath my sails
She makes me feel ten feet tall

I think I may be Superman
I feel the world is my hands
Can I get lost in her dreamland

Mistake

There was a broken promise
There was a broken trust
I said I would never leave
You said you'd never give up

All that was never said
Sits here cold in this
Unmade bed

A vanishing soul
On an empty chair
Sitting here
Wishing you where there

Careless with each moment
Hands rough to the touch
I know I took you for granted
I'm sorry just isn't enough

How love is remembered
So strong in our lust
You gave me your heart
And I ripped it up

And all I know now
All I can say
Is that I love you and
That I made a mistake

Be Myself

Through your eyes love is shinning
Even though it might seem blinding
Light reflects the lovers flame
In your eyes I see no shame

You accept me as I am
My heart you hold in your hands
Sweetly like notes to a song
Forever like this our love goes on

I see myself with you

No more hiding behind closed doors
The window opens now like never before
Like circle to square that has no place
A perfect fit you fill my space

My heart's rhythm has found its song
My naked abandoned my shyness gone
Water floods and flows through me
A safe oasis where we can be

I see myself in you

Everything inside of me
I have value and am worthy of being
I believe that what you say is true
Love calls to me in the form of you

I can see myself, be myself and that is something new
Never as free as when I am lovingly lost with you
Rooted in a truth that hiding just won't do

I see myself and you

That's It That's All

I found love across a crowded room
Saw you sitting there and lost my sound
I caught your eyes and felt my soul
If I was still dancing, I did not know
Control was given to you by no fault of my own
Could only hear my own heartbeat
Vision went soft, focus lost
I loved you, that's it -- that's all…

A fool, I found my voice had a mind of its own
Me without choice not all who wander roam
My life spoken to you in song, word, and rhyme
Masks intertwining future coming while at the
Same time confronting past but instead of passing
You bye, a collision of passion, jet plane fast
Barley enough time to take a breath, water rising
An oasis of protection, a puzzle of pieces, running away
Escaping that which is inevitable, these souls
Connecting through the mesh made into walls
I loved you, that's it -- that's all…

Split apart at the beginning of time
Long time searching an epic herstory to find
A million different lifetimes lived, many loves
Many twists, many tries, how many times
How many trips did it take us to finally find
One another again, too many trips around the sun
Only now to sit at its setting holding hands
A lifetime later to once again
I loved you, that's it – this is the one

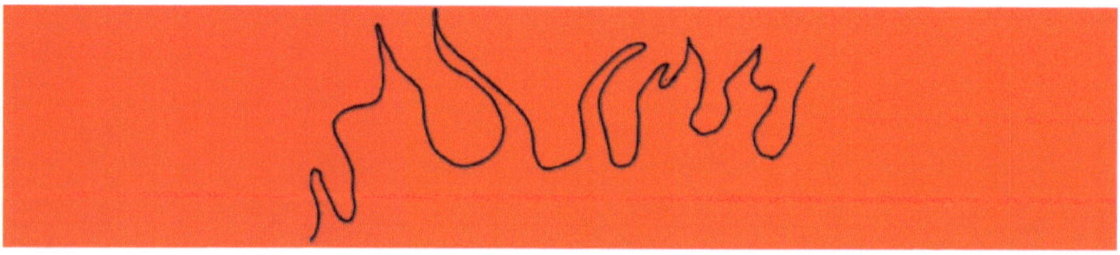

Laid Bare

Been There

LIAR, LIAR, your ass is on fire!
Pained with a desire
To seem more than what you are

Falling, failing, the depths of waiting
How far – Wow far
Will you go to hide the scar
That shows so presently on your face
Well-fitted mask of insecurity and disgrace

Whatever you are -- I am
Whatever you've seen -- I've seen
Wherever you've been -- I've been
Whatever you've done -- I've done

Who are we
What have we become
Of me there is nothing left
I am whatever you say I am
DAMN…

The whole only gets deeper
I only become weaker

Fear has become my life
I am the only speaker

Perceptive

The Hips
The Lips
The Walk
The Talk
The Look
The Life

Butch or Femme
Male of Female
Or something in between

Unknown
Unfathomable
Unseen

It all entails
Perception prevails

You see me and you automatically think
No lipstick, no dress, no hair
She don't care

Does the book match the cover
Or is the cover just a cover

Because it's not the right skin
She's in

Perception is thin
Open the book, delve within

She be thick with language and sense
Intense and deep
Their own mystique

The clothes don't make the man
The womyn makes the clothes look good

When your perception of what a womyn should be
Releases you from disbelief

Then you will finally be able to see me!

CRACKS

No more darkness and still all is black
You're the only light I want
The only light I can see

Even still with a shaking hand
I pour you down the sink
Because with you
I cannot be

In reality
The hole in the sink
Is not saying
Drink me
Drink me

Waiting for The Unknown

We Give Birth Astride a Grave

Two slits in my back
Open like vertical eyelids

Blood stains the body
Clothes shred to nothing

Exploding

I Expand

Every fowl of the air
And winged thing

Yielding from me
Multiplying the seed
Inside thyself

Idolatry as Fame

LIKE a loaded gun we are about to go off
A world of ignorance surrounds us
And we are pissed off!

Everything we have inside us
Will satisfy everything we need

Yet we look for it outside ourselves
Like mad, ravenous, fiends

Idols impede our clear thinking
Control our wanting, feeling, even dreaming

Language is convoluted
Authority figures are polluted

Human Nature is transmuted
Our minds are diluted

BANG! BANG! BANG!

Expose the IDOLS, Break the Chains!

The National Nation

When did peace become unpatriotic,
America the beautiful?
Home of the free and the brave

Built on bloody broken backs
Native Americans
Invisible Immigrants
Forgotten Slaves

Imaginary pedestal
Of stolen power
Preach to the world
How they should live
Follow our illustrious lead

Forget the Unforgettable
Be proud of our country
Hide behind the burning bush
Revising despicable acts

Letting blatant lies perpetuate in our children's schoolbooks

Ameri can't change the world

Excuse Me

Slowing moving inch by inch
Limbs making mockery of molasses

Shadows like heavy burdens
Block my path

Future lying in wait
Covered by past

Thoughts
Dreams
Daemons
Feigning Thieves

Biting at the bit of my heels
Keeping me from creating things

Holding onto breaking branches
Destroying roots of living things

Unable to fly, breathing used air
Coughing up smoke
Beginning to choke
Getting scared

A tunnel without light at either end
Holding onto a circle trying not to bend

Too tight – too lose
Traveling without end

Footsteps that follow
Footsteps that lead

Hearing footsteps in the dark
Chasing me as I'm

Chasing everything

Can't seem to get out of my own way… Say excuse me!

T
H
I
S

TIM**E**

What **D**o **I** **A**lways **W**ish **T**o **R**emember **F**rom **T**his **T**ime
What I always wish to **R**emember is that which I can **N**ever **F**orget…
The sadness in my heart
The struggle for basic humanity that tears apart the muscle of my soul

The lack of understanding for the life of another human being screaming for validation and love into an unrequited void
A light in the darkened cave of my mind
The forest through the trees that our society has conditioned us not to see and when we do so call us blind

A moment of recognition and relief

A moment - just to breathe… Just to breathe… JUST. TO. BREATHE….

Our hearts cry out in a world of violence - please a moment of peace!
The repetition of this fucked up dehumanizing life condition…
Damn, this feels familiar…. Have I been here before?

I have a sinking feeling this is not new, for so many battles that have been won – we are still in the same war

I want to **R**emember:
Those who came before us
Those we have left behind
Those whose lives were cut short
Those still waiting in line
Those on the forefront

Those on the backburner

Those whose lives we honor like **T**ubman, **K**ing and **T**urner
Those lost in the shuffle
Those ready to cause trouble
Those who sing out loud
Those voices lost in the crowd
Those whose eyes pierce your soul
Those **Y**oung – **F**earless and **B**old
Those **O**lder, **W**ise and **R**esolute
Those finger on the trigger ready to shoot
Those **A**ngry, **I**solated and **A**fraid
Those who cannot speak ---- whose bodies fill up with **RAGE**
Those who lost the opportunity to AGE

Those who love beyond all comprehension and measure – where love does not exist for them – they become loves treasures

Those who pray with their entire being and forgive the unforgivable
Those who hold their heads high with a knee on their neck

Those who bow their heads daily and are still not given one ounce of respect

Those that have never given up after years and years – struggle after struggle – test after test, they continue to rise from every piece of burning ash as a PHEONIX and in the position of the thinking man ask – **WHAT'S NEXT!**

Those who rest in Power
Those who fight for Peace
Those who exist just to make it through another day

Those who get lost in a foggy daze – drugs the only way to release… My Uncle still in Prison to this day for the crime of trying to find PEACE!

Those whose mental stability broken by a system of abuse
Those labelled harmful for this world failed to find them of use

Those so abused by this land they called MOTHER… where the only thing taught was to abuse one another

Those who lie in wait
Those who fight to educate
Those told to be quiet
Those told to hold on

Those told to act right and be proper for you won't have to wait toooooooo long

Those who **LAUGH** ManiacallY
Those who **STAND** DefiantlY
Those whose deaths have spawned a change in our society

I always want to **R**emember whose lives we valued best

If we are to improve this is our **LAST** and **F**inal **TEST**
Those whose constant sacrifice is also their constant abuse
Those who ask for equality and not revenge… don't think twice
Those who use their privilege to break down a system that only benefits them…
Is.   More.   Than.   Being.   Nice!

Those who died from a **V**irus that shined a light on incompetence and inequity within – too much sacrificed

Those giving of themselves to those in need
Those holding the line
Those that **BLEED**
Those who take the time to plant, water and nurture new young seeds
Those who take a moment to confirm before they blindly just believe
Those who break their own personal bubble and awaken to the true reality

Those who understand the value of every **H**uman **B**eing

Those who refuse to be QUIET

Those who refuse to **S**uffer in SILENCE - about the truth of what a black life really means

I want to **Remember**… less we repeat ourselves again

I want to Remember, that I was here at the Eleventh hour, when…

Because We Are One

To be in your body
To stand in your dreams
To let your breath well up inside you
To exhale power unseen

What comes to life blossoms in the mud
To create beauty in the midst of all the madness we see

Horns are blaring, people are staring, lights are flashing, cars are crashing

We hear but we don't listen
We look but we don't see

People sell themselves as art
To shed their skin and fall apart
Just to be born again

What part do I play
What is this we are in

To be in my body
To stand in my dreams
To let breath well up inside me
To exhale power unseen

I am the beauty that blossoms in the mud
We cannot give up until we are one

Heavy

In heavy darkness
Light still breaks through
When your eyes finally adjust to see
That truths have always been hidden

We wear a different mask for each emotion of the day
We finally hear the scream that shakes us awake
Don't go, the darkness calls

Wind howling like monkeys in the night
Fight or flight, we determine to make it through the longest rite

Like passengers who forgot to forget
We sing the song of the indecent, ferocious, crazy malcontents
And still, with the appropriate amount of intent
We insist and behest
We beg for better days
Yet we are victim to dangers from which we run

A test we forgot to study for
Yet were inherently born to pass
We made it unbearable for the unbreakable
At last, we find ourselves not the first and foremost
But the dash between a forgotten memory and a broken dream

A wish, a wish upon, a wish upon a star…

Mystery and memory mixed like painted faces
On a canvas of bleeding
Falling leaves of all the trees our expectations were hung upon

Everything about our lives
Incorrectly drawn

Not the last note
But a beautiful harmony
Of all who have come and gone…

Living On

Mornin' they all say
As the bell sounds
They come to work
The fields
The barns
The houses
The hills
The tracks
Broken backs
For who
They kill themselves; not for themselves

To give, and give, and give
Until there is nothing left
Even more of themselves
They endeavor to give
For pleasure
For pain
For fear
For God
For country
For love
For me
The meek shall inherit the earth
As the earth inherits me

Oh Mable, oh Maddie, oh May
Come o'er here girl! You have no name
Your birthright and your shame
Come clean my house for free
No Irish, No Blacks, no Dogs
No BIPOC, LGBTQ+, No humanity at all
And the meek still live on

My my it's nippy out today
Man, do you even here what you say

As they break their backs to make roads for your way
Man do you even hear what you say

The Indians, the Braves, The Chiefs, or The Slaves
As we pay our money to watch the barbarians play
Continually contributing to ruin a great heritage, a good name

What are your reservations
Things held back or unsaid
For fear they may haunt you one day
The reservations in your mind
Or the reservations back in time
Where you watched Cowboys and Indians play
Please, our reservations
We're going to be a little late

Ignorant moments of treachery
Microaggressions on repeated play
The abused, the abuser, the victim, the accuser
Easily taking each other's place
Live on, nothing's wrong, every day all day

Believe In Me

Beauty believed when she saw me
That I was something beautiful to see
I could not believe her
For beauty was not real to me

Beauty as the eye of the beholder
I could not stand the beholding of me
For the beholding was a controlling
Of what they wanted me to be

A darkness that rolled around inside
A sick and broken lie
For it touched me and groped me with its
Leering eyes, sick tongue, and gyrating thighs

How could I see beauty
An ugly thing I tried to be
If this was Beauty then she
Would be no part of me

It would take time for me to see
That beauty was mine and
Only belonged to me

It would take time to breathe and release
It would take time to find wholeness and peace
It would take time to unclench my fists
It would take time to know more than this
It would take time to take murder off my list

When Beauty found me again
This time I gave her a kiss
For Beauty recognizes beauty
And together we realized this

Cycle

Wished it
never was
yet it had always
broken through

A dream
a team
a wicked thing
that I never
admitted was true

The enemy
afraid to see
a nightmare
in the daytime
chasing me

Allowed it to grow
it started to show
then I knew
not what to do

Told it no, still
It would not go

Pushed away
dark thoughts
tried to fight it
still right through
me and onto you

Wish it had not
fought for it to stop
but too little was I
when it found you

Apologize
tears in my eyes
seeing the nightmare
come to life
then to see you

Family of mine
lost in so much time
next in the firing line
now I give my life
to save you

Wish so much
that I was braver
a big sister
a hero
a savior

Instead, darkness
covered you
so much like me
even more than
I was you

For life as it stands
I see this new plan
thriving and true
not crushed by the past
victorious at last

Victim no more
the battle scars worn
survivors like me and you
vast inequities and
complexities
unfortunately, past down
from me to you

I will no more
let evil through
that door, so now
I send only light to you

As Me…

Children, never give up and never be defeated
That's how one wins the day

Always believed it so never retreated
That's how we managed to stay

Beaten over and under and down again
We knew no other way

In the reflection of eyes young and old
A terrible history continues to play

We passed it down and turned it around
That's how we are still here this day

Fearing nothing in our way
Emerging, resurging, and constantly un-learning

Children learn by watching, times not stopping
So, mind what we are teaching in the daily roles we play

Mimicking the madness, wallowing in sadness
Giving up or not following through

A ridiculous thing to continue after so many things
That we have already broken through

Be meticulous in the interest of those who look up to you
Children hear what we say but do what we do

Each one, teach one, is always something true
Children, never feel as if you are not heard

Because, as me, I SEE you…

Time

So much so little
a vestibule hidden
outside of a riddle

Intertwined and drenched
in wine that was once
cared for, now brittle

An observant owl
a lifetime of looks
on a branch, perfectly
imprinted talons

No longer has time
aged and beautiful
wisdom filled and
life defiant

Take time to listen
a book closed
not yet retired
still trying to find
what has lost the mind

A world no longer compliant
limbs not listening
memory no longer remembering
skin no longer glistening
trying hard to fight it

Time is not a question
clock arms never turn back
the second of the second hand
creates an incredibly intricate map
always searching for which X
marks the spot to get back

NO

NO, I said…
As I covered the blankets over myself and hid underneath my bed

NO, I said…
As I blocked your hand from covering my mouth and bit you instead

NO, I said…
As you laid yourself on top of me and I pretended I was dead

NO, I said…
As pants unbuttoned and zippers unzipped, and I felt a wetness on my head

NO, I said…
As I heard footsteps outside my bedroom door and the sound of the locked being picked kept ringing in my head

NO, I said…
As cold, clammy hands found their way up to my warm body in the safety of my absent stead

NO, I said…
As I was locked in an embrace unable to move, crowded in your space, unable to speak, my voice and spirit away chased

NO, I said…
Wanting to scream it wildly out loud but so frozen with fear and disgust it only came out in my head

NO, I said…
Pretending to be sleep as I waited for you a knife underneath my pillow hoping to bleed you instead

NO, I said…

For every woman ever violated, disrespected, misused, misread, abused, discounted, and left for dead

NO, I said…
That once is enough for if I have to say it again the wrath of every woman in every time that ever lived will murder you in every waking hour and haunt you a million times until you are forever dead

NO, I SAID. I SAID NO!

What then...

Empty shoes sit in the middle of the street. A road towards a vanishing point with no end, and as each step is taken another story begins. The multiverse of a multitude of all the universes within. Three thousand realms in a single moment without beginning or end. Empty shoes that carried the life of many more that could be expressed. Empty shoes are empty because they had nothing left, nothing more to do and nothing more to say, empty shoes that with toes exposed and frayed tried to tell a story but instead walked in silence that day.

In the middle of the road there lay an empty pair of shoes. Weren't sure if they came down from the line above or were just old and no longer of good use. Was someone snatched out of them before anyone could, see? Maybe these shoes tell a story of someone long deceased. These shoes could have been cast aways of feet needing to be free. Swollen, beaten, lost, and defeated, feet that just needed space. Maybe there are a new pair of shoes enjoying life that have taken empty shoes' place.

Empty shoe has traveled far and wide to make it here this day. Once it is witnessed it cannot be undone and if the shoe cannot tell its own story, then it will be made up of one. Nothing stands alone, and nothing can be out of place. The history of his – story is always being undone and when the truth is realized about the empty shoes, we may realize what never was. For the empty shoes standing in the middle of the street where not so empty at all. The person wearing them went by unnoticed, invisible to us all.

Picture This

It's not the loud and screaming,
the belligerent, and malcontent
No, it is the quiet, the thoughtful, and the unassuming
you should be mindful of and be careful not to miss

If you are ignorant enough to believe your evil deeds
are not on someone's list,
Be careful of your arrogance, as it will hit you
when you least expect something could be amiss

Under your bed, in your head, a dream you forgot
to forget and then something akin to a nightmare
that follows you like this:
The monster you created is the one that waits and sits

And when it's time, and it will always be time,
that monster will surely check you off their list
For that which is taken must always be repaid
So, make sure you remember this:
What you do to others will most certainly be returned
in kind so be mindful of the reaction to your most base action
for this is a struggle for power you cannot win

When you are ready to face your maker,
it is in the mirror you should look for
every piece and peace you thoughtlessly and violently took
A piece of you is missing and therein lies the hook
The broken, missing pieces of a puzzle unfinished
should have you shook, for soon enough
there will be nothing left for the hole you were trying to fill
is the hole that holds your death

Champion

He is our weapon you say
What an interesting choice
Speaking about a young Black man

Afterall, we are talking about a game that people play
A human being is not a weapon
And life is not a game

A weapon is to be feared not revered
It is wielded and controlled
Aimed at; designed to destroy

This beautiful young Black man
Full of power, grace, and poise
Using his skills, his brain to achieve field goals

He is our Champion you should say
The best of all of us
On any given Sunday

If winning on the field is your only goal
And Black bodies are commodities
Recruited, bought and sold…

Then your winning streak should end

Unnecessary

Sitting next to you I am annoyed

Your voice so wretched
The mere presence of you steals my joy

In a theatre after COVID
How dare you sit right next to me?

So much space yet you find yourself
And your ass closer than they need to be

You take up so much space, why and how in this day and age
Have you still not realized your place?

We have had to put up with you for far too long
You're ignorant and arrogant and still you ask for grace!

Not knowing how to say excuse me, thinking every conversation you have
Is one we should all pay attention to

Quiet yourself and move to the left with your
Loud unnecessary breath

How much fucking attention do you really need?
How long must we continue to acquiesce?

Shut the fuck up! Sit the fuck down! And finally realize your place
And understand… You have never been the only game in town!

The Gift

Clear and present
Dangerous at my best
Rising above the fray
Preparing for what is inevitably next

One step to the next
One foot passing the other
One door opening
The first of many obstacles, I came over

One mountain at a time
The arduous climb
That never give up spirit
I had to find

Never give up
Never again
Will I ever allow
Fear, foolishness, and laziness to win

Honesty first
No strategy before me
I am my only obstacle
Myself thine own feared enemy

Try me if you will
On site if you must
Understand who you are talking to
For what I have come through, trust

You will never know another
No not like me
For if you ever walked in my shoes
You would be frightened by what you see

Though maybe you should be

You would likely look at me differently
Understand that there is purpose to my peace
For the opposite of that is nothing you want to see

Up from almost drowning
Raised from the dead
Healed from horrific wounds
Constant pain in my head

If what does not kill me
Makes me stronger
Then I am stronger still
Stronger than that which tries to defeat me

Stronger than your will
Stronger than that which can be tested measured, or read
Stronger than I think, stronger than I feel, strong enough
Victorious against all that would wish me ill

I am the lotus flower that blossoms in the mud
The rose that grows from concrete
The medicine made from the disease
The hope you cannot see

I am that which was made from pressure
Pressing against itself, a fire in the hole
Through intense heat, I broke the mold
One of nature's most incredible and unique gifts

The Eleventh Hour

The eleventh hour has come at last
Are we too late, has it come too fast

Are we ready to answer for all we have done
Should we wait, see, or should we run

The last stretch, trying to fix all we messed
We want to continue
Self-preservation a test we should have passed

Took too long to study
Forgot to read all the instructions
Answered the questions too fast

Can we repay a debt of gratitude we never knew we had?
What we took for granted can we seriously ask for it back?

Do we think we are owed or deserve a second chance
Would we use or abuse?
Our pattern permeates our past

Can we learn from our past mistakes repetition our final fate
All the transgressions on our slate
The state we find ourselves in now

Apologies, too little too late
We couldn't even care for our own kind
Bastardized nature, took her for granted
Why should she save us now?

If we knew better, we would have come together
Seeing how weak we are now
Stronger united, but we stay divided
Still can't figure out how

If this is the end of our story, our final fate foretold

A simulation of what life could be
If we endeavor to change nothing
The eleventh hour holds

Emerging

Clarity seen through an empty glass
Still life escapes me
I tried to break free
Yet it's my jaded past that
That holds me down under

I can barely breathe
Through all this skin
That is coloring me
The different parts of me

Leave me alone
Trying to tell me
Who you think I am becoming
Controlling every part of me

Everyone gets their chance
We all take our shots
Sometimes we're made to feel
That we won't amount to much

Don't take it to heart
Or believe everything you hear
Don't drink what they give you
Their water is not so clear

We all have judgements
Mostly it's the mirrors
Reflected in our eyes
That's why we cry

We all have sadness
And will encounter struggles
Until the day we die
That's sometimes why we hide

If each person could turn
And truly look at the other
They'd discover all the different parts
Uniquely connected

www.ingramcontent.com/pod-product-compliance
Lightning Source LLC
Chambersburg PA
CBHW042334150426
43194CB00005B/160